MILITARY DOGS

EMILY SCHLESINGER

NONFICTION

Area 51
Bioweapons
Cannibal Animals
Cloning
Comet Catcher
Drones
Fault Lines
Gnarly Sports Injuries
Great Spies of the World
Hacked
Little Rock Nine
Medal of Honor
Military Dogs
Monsters of the Deep
Monsters on Land
The Science of Movies
Seven Wonders of the Ancient World
3D Printing
Tuskegee Airmen
Virtual Reality
Wild Weather
Witchcraft
Wormholes
Zombie Creatures

Photo credits: cover and page 2/3: Nate Derrick / Shutterstock.com; page 10: Science History Images / Alamy Stock Photo; page 12/13: Stocktrek Images, Inc. / Alamy Stock Photo; page 28/29: 615 collection / Alamy Stock Photo; page 32/33: US Air Force Photo / Alamy Stock Photo; page 36/37: National Geographic Creative / Alamy Stock Photo; page 36/37: Stocktrek Images, Inc. / Alamy Stock Photo; page 42/43: Stocktrek Images, Inc. / Alamy Stock Photo; 44/45: PA Images / Alamy Stock Photo; page 48/49: US Air Force Photo / Alamy Stock Photo; All other source images from Shutterstock.com

ISBN-13: 978-1-68021-075-0
ISBN-10: 1-68021-075-0
eBook: 978-1-63078-383-9

Printed in Malaysia

23 22 21 20 19   2 3 4 5 6

TABLE OF CONTENTS

Chapter 1
THE SOLDIER

It happened behind closed doors.
A secret group met.
They were at a military base.
Fort Campbell was the name.
No press could come in.

The President was there.
It was Barack Obama.
Joe Biden was there too.
He was the VP.

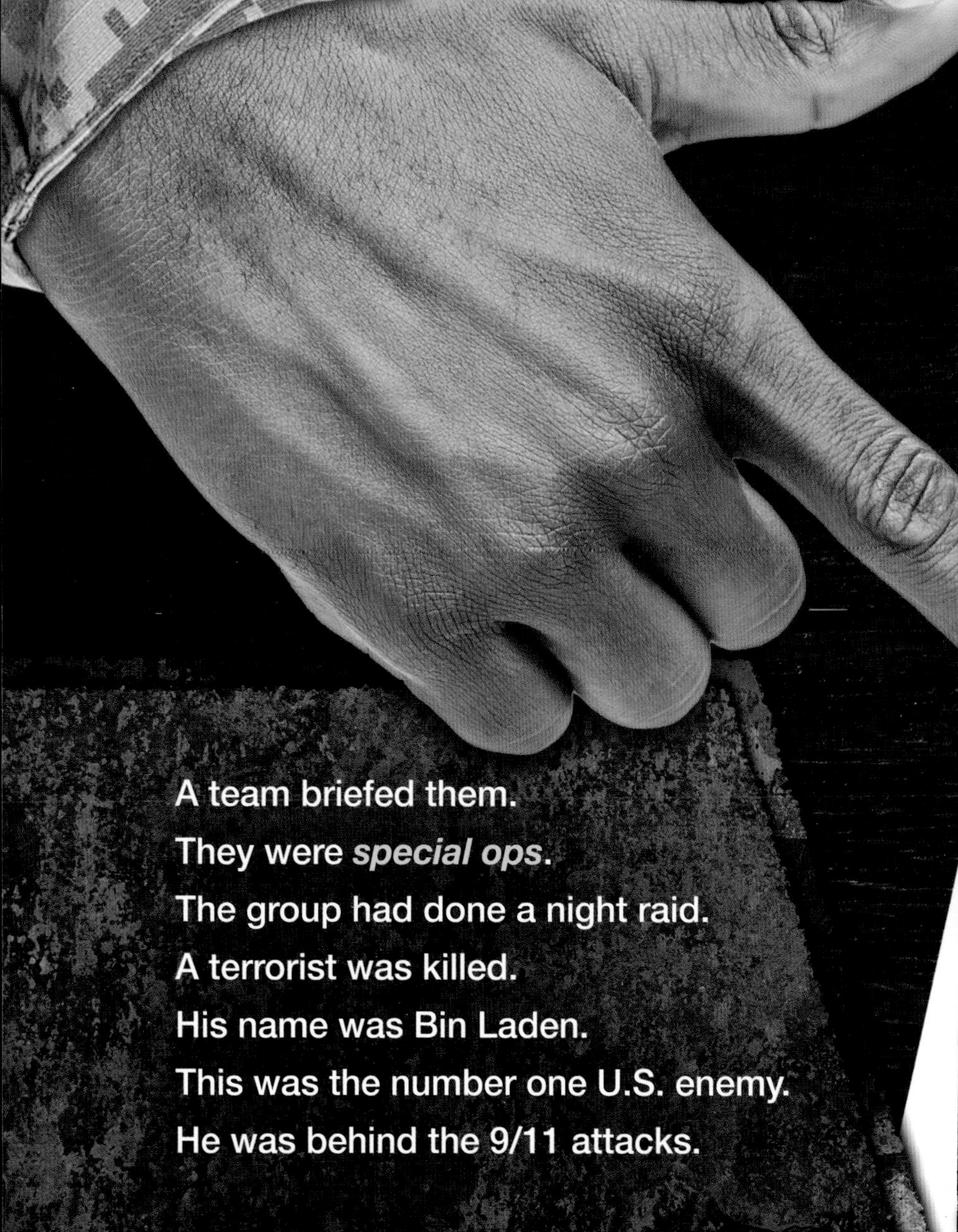

A team briefed them.
They were *special ops*.
The group had done a night raid.
A terrorist was killed.
His name was Bin Laden.
This was the number one U.S. enemy.
He was behind the 9/11 attacks.

It was a big win.
The President wanted to give an award.
But the team had to stay secret.

WWW.REDRHINOBOOKS.COM

9781680210750

9781680210286

9781680210309

9781680210507

9781680210354

9781680210736

9781680210521

9781680210361

9781680210514

9781680210323

9781680210330

9781680210743

9781680210767

MORE TITLES COMING SOON

K9 TRIVIA

SEALs take part in secret missions. The Bin Laden mission was code-named "Operation Neptune Spear."

6

Only one hero's name was given.
This was an *elite* soldier.
He was a highly trained expert.
His job was complex.
In fact, he helped lead the raid.

The soldier was brought in.
The President rose.
He placed an arm on his shoulder.
Then he looked into his eyes.
"Job well done," he said.

The President thanked him for his service.
He praised his heroic deeds.
And then he stroked his fur.
The hero was a dog.

Chapter 2
CAIRO

The dog's name is Cairo.
He is a Belgian ***breed***.
His unit is the SEALs.
This stands for "Sea, Air, and Land."
It is part of the Navy.

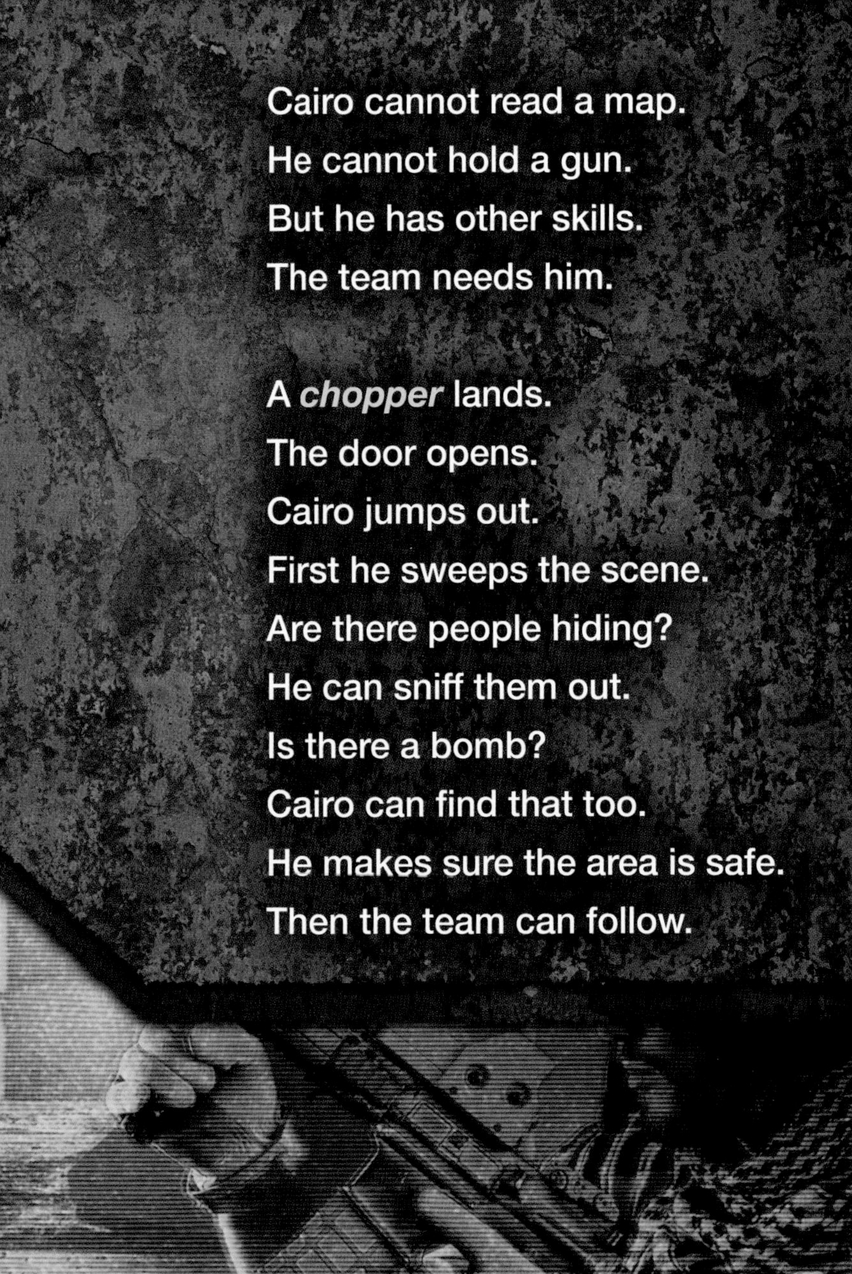

Cairo cannot read a map.
He cannot hold a gun.
But he has other skills.
The team needs him.

A *chopper* lands.
The door opens.
Cairo jumps out.
First he sweeps the scene.
Are there people hiding?
He can sniff them out.
Is there a bomb?
Cairo can find that too.
He makes sure the area is safe.
Then the team can follow.

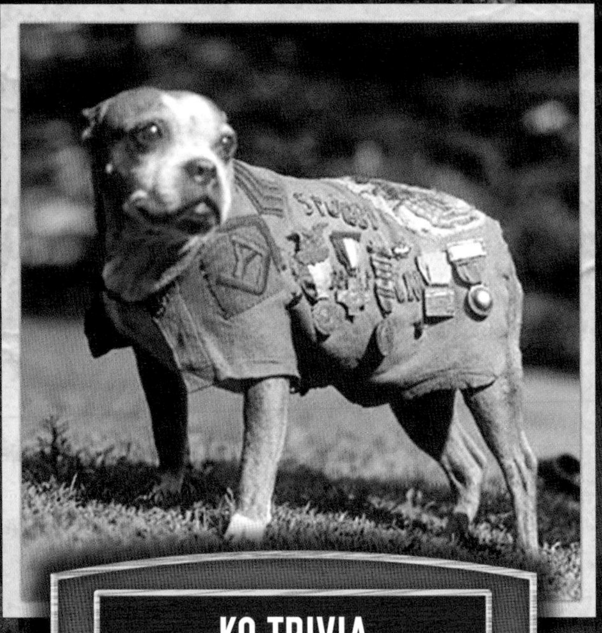

K9 TRIVIA

The first famous dog war hero was named Sergeant Stubby. He warned troops of a gas attack during World War I.

Cairo wears a camera.
It records video.
This is sent to the team.
He also wears goggles.
They give him night vision.
He can see through walls.

Cairo wears a suit.
It keeps him safe.
This is state of the art.
It cost $86,000.
But Cairo is worth it.
He is an important part of the team.

Chapter 3
DOGS IN THE MILITARY

Up to 3,000 dogs serve in the military.
That is just in the U.S.
The Army and Navy have them.
The *Marines* do too.
Many work at sea.
They help the Coast Guard.

Dogs sniff out dangers.
They search for people.
Some gather *intel*.
Others attack targets.

K9 TRIVIA

America's military dogs often come from Europe. Top breeds are German Shepherds and Belgian Malinois.

They can *parachute* jump too.
Cara does.
She dove from 30,000 feet.
That is as high as a jet flies.
It set a record for a dog.

Cara jumped with her teacher.
His name is Mike.
She wore a K9 Storm vest.
It holds a parachute.
Cara wore oxygen too.
Air is thin up there.

It may seem strange to parachute with a dog.
But troops must get to places quickly.
Flying in might be the only way.

Chapter 4
A DOG'S NOSE

Think about your nose.
What if it was 100 times stronger?
A dog would still have a better nose.
It can smell 100,000 times better.

Here is an example.
Take a drop of sweat.
Spread it over a whole city.
A dog would notice it.

Dogs can pick apart smells too.
Picture a birthday party.
You smell a cake.
What does a dog smell?
It smells flour, eggs, and sugar.
Each part stands out.
Humans do not have this skill.

K9 TRIVIA

Dogs learn to smell ingredients that are used in bombs and weapons.

A DOG'S NOSE

Air flows out

Air flows in

Chapter 5
SCOUTING

This ability to smell is important in war.
A bomb may be near.
Or it could be a land *mine*.
Troops have no idea where.
But a dog can smell it.

Sniffing out threats is called scouting.
This is a dog's biggest strength.
It saves lives.

Cali was a scout.
She worked in the Army.
Her job was to sniff.
She found traps and mines.
Snipers could be around too.

Cali worked with a man.
His name was Larry.
One day they were walking.
Cali stopped.
Larry thought something was wrong.
He called his commander.
Soldiers searched.
But they found nothing.
The commander told him to keep going.

Soon Cali stopped again.
This time, Larry felt sure.
Something was wrong.
Again he called.
His commander was firm.
"The men found no threat," he said.
"You must keep going."
It was an order.

Larry faced a choice.
He could not turn down an order.
That could get him fired.
It would be a crime.

But Larry trusted Cali.
He believed in her nose.
Larry knew he was breaking rules.
But he said no to his commander.
He let Cali lead instead.

It was a life-saving move.
There was an enemy ambush.
It was just around the bend.
Cali knew.
She warned them.
They all could have died.
But Larry listened.

K9 TRIVIA

Cali and 4,000 other dogs served in the Vietnam War. They saved over 10,000 lives.

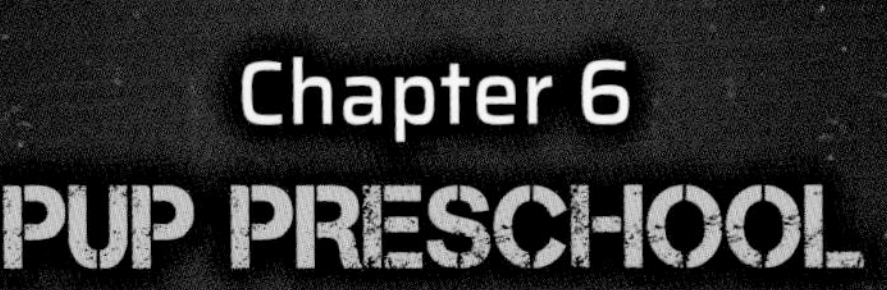

Chapter 6
PUP PRESCHOOL

Soldier dogs need many skills.
They must be strong.
Smarts are a must.
Things cannot get under their skin.
They have to be friendly too.

Training starts young.
A pup gets tests.
Someone tickles its toes.
Does the pup stay calm?
They might hold the pup upside down.
Is it trusting?
These are signs.
They show ***personality***.

Not all puppies pass.
But many do.
These go to a ***foster family***.
Kids in the family can help.
They teach early skills.
Being social is one.
Pups learn to get along with others.

Families take them on errands too.
This helps them get used to new places.
It makes pups well-rounded.
Some call it pup preschool.

K9 TRIVIA

When puppies are about 7 months old, they are ready for real military training.

Chapter 7
TRAINING TIME

Human soldiers go to boot camp to train.
So do dogs.
It is like boarding school.
They say goodbye to their families.
Training lasts many months.

First, dogs learn to ***patrol***.
This takes practice.
A person plays the enemy.
They wear a suit.
It is called a bite suit.
This protects them from dog teeth.

K9 TRIVIA

Dogs are trained at Lackland Air Force Base in San Antonio, Texas, as part of the Military Working Dog Program.

ALLEN

Next, dogs learn *scents*.
It may seem like work.
But to dogs it is a game.
They run after a smell.
Then they sit.
Did they get it right?
That calls for a treat.
It makes them want to try again.
They get this over time.

Dogs also learn what to expect.
They practice going on aircraft.
Trainers take them into strange buildings.
The dogs get used to loud sounds.
Gunfire is one.
Soon they are not afraid.

Chapter 8
ON DUTY

It is time for duty.
The dog goes to a base.
It works with a ***handler***.
This is a soldier.
They train together.
Both have a ***rank***.
But the dog's rank is one higher.
This is for a reason.
The soldier must always respect the dog.

Chris is a handler.
His dog is Kira.
The two were sent to Afghanistan.
They helped a special ops team.
Kira found ***IEDs***.
These are a type of bomb.
"I take pride," Chris said.
"While Kira and I were out working, my guys did not get blown up."

The two took care of each other.
Chris would scratch her belly.
He rubbed her foot pads.
Chris explained why.
"She was out there making sure we were safe.
It wasn't much in return for what she did."

The troops loved Kira.
She joined them at the campfire.
They would slip her food.
She slept on a board.
One man felt bad about this.
He bought her a new bed.
It was memory foam.

Soldiers like dogs at camp.
They help with ***stress***.
And it is less lonely.
But handlers have the strongest ***bond***.
They are always with their dogs.
It is a 24-hour job.

War is stressful.
Every day is life or death.
Both soldier and dog face fears.
They depend on one another.
Their bond grows.
"Once that bond is formed, it's unbreakable," Chris said.

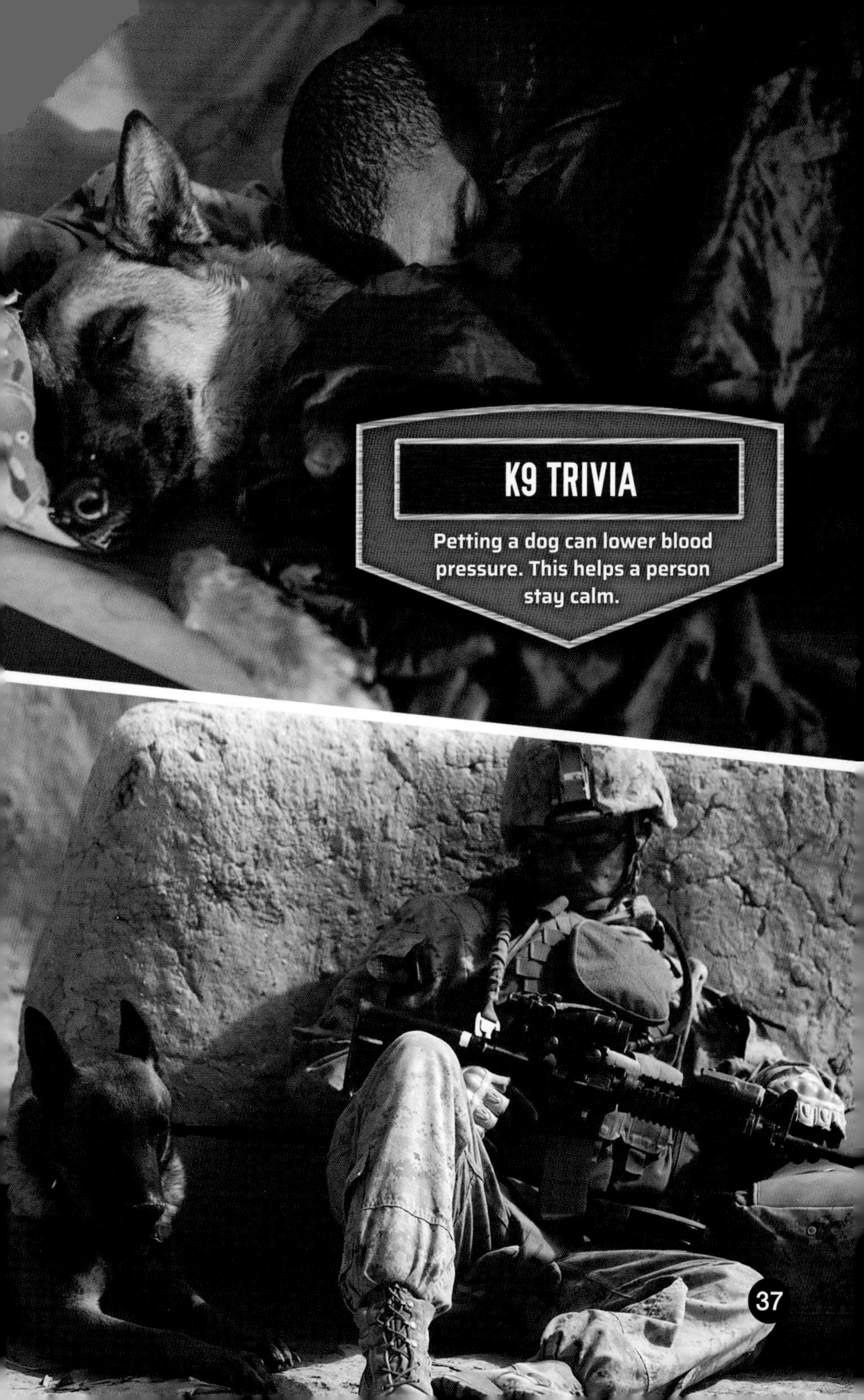

K9 TRIVIA

Petting a dog can lower blood pressure. This helps a person stay calm.

Chapter 9
A CLOSE BOND

Dogs work hard.
They serve for years.
But even dogs *retire*.
People adopt them.

Colton was a handler.
Eli was his dog.
They had a close bond.

The two were always a pair.
Eli slept in Colton's sleeping bag.

The camp had a chow hall.
Dogs were not allowed in.
So Colton ate outside.
He wanted to be with Eli.
"Whatever is mine is his," Colton said.

NO
DOGS

K9 TRIVIA

When military dogs retire, their handler gets first dibs. Most of the time, they go home to live with the handler. If not, they can be adopted by other families. The wait list to adopt retired military dogs is very long.

One day they were shot at.
It was sniper fire.
Eli crawled on top of Colton to protect him.
Other soldiers saw it.
Eli made a shield.
But Colton did not live.

Colton's family adopted Eli.
He reminds them of their son.
"Eli was a part of Colton," his grandma said.

Chapter 10
HEROES

War is dangerous.
Troops help one another.
They do anything for each other.
Dogs are the same way.
Both humans and dogs face risks.
They make *sacrifices*.

Lucca did.
She was a Marine.
Her service lasted six years.
She went on more than 400 missions.
Lucca was a top patrol dog too.
No one died on her watch.

One day an IED went off.
Lucca was hurt.
Her handler rushed over.
He helped her right away.
"She had saved my life," he said.
"I had to make sure that I was there for her."
Lucca lived.
But her leg was removed.

Lucca was given an honor.
It was the Dickin Medal.
This is for brave service.
It is the highest an animal can get.

DICKIN MEDAL

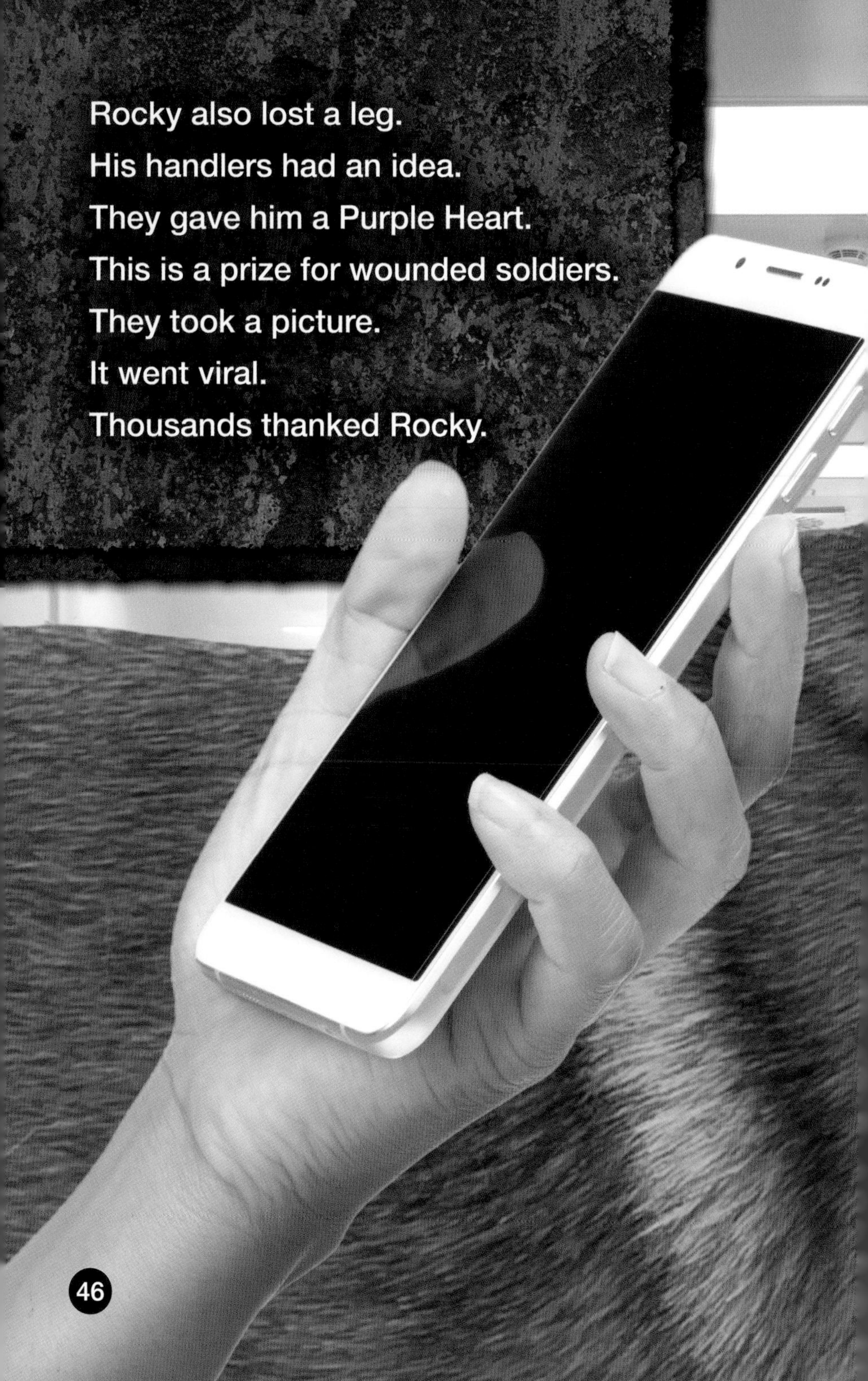

Rocky also lost a leg.
His handlers had an idea.
They gave him a Purple Heart.
This is a prize for wounded soldiers.
They took a picture.
It went viral.
Thousands thanked Rocky.

Dogs have proven themselves.
They are brave heroes.
Their skills are second to none.
They lift hearts.
And they save lives.
That is why even presidents say thank you.

GLOSSARY

bond: a feeling of closeness

breed: a certain kind of dog

chopper: helicopter

elite: part of a high-level group

foster family: people who take care of someone for a limited time

handler: a person who trains and takes care of an animal

IED: a simple or homemade bomb

intel: information helpful to the military

Marine: a branch of the military

mine: a bomb that goes off when touched

parachute: a cloth that fills with air to allow a safe fall from great heights

patrol: to guard and protect

personality: what someone tends to act like

rank: a title that tells one's place in the military

retire: stop working at a job

sacrifice: a choice to give up something valuable in service to a cause

scent: a specific smell

sniper: someone who shoots from a hiding place or a high place, like a rooftop

special ops: a military team that is highly trained to meet a goal

stress: the feeling of being alert or tense

TAKE A LOOK INSIDE

ZOMBIE CREATURES

Chapter 4
DANCE OF DEATH
Another worm has the same goal.
It must get into a bird too.
That is where it will reproduce.
But it has a different trick.
CREEPY FACT
Gliding ants live in trees. When they fall, they glide gently to safety.
A gliding ant helps.
The ant eats the worm's eggs.
They hatch in its backside.
The ant's rear swells.
It looks like a ripe, red berry.
18
19

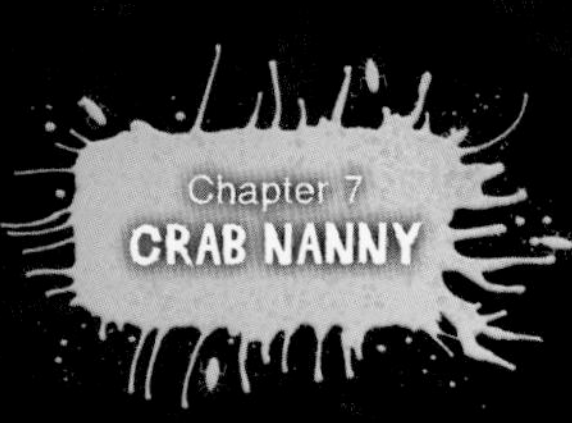

Parasites don't stop at mind control.
Some go further.
The *barnacle* is one.
This creature is tiny.
It lives in the sea.

The barnacle meets a crab.
Then it sheds its shell.
It crawls into the crab's claw.
What does the barnacle want?
Its young need care.
The crab will help.
It just doesn't know it yet.

CREEPY FACT

A barnacle parasite looks like an egg yolk stuck to the crab.

BARNACLE

How does it get from rat to cat?
A cat could eat the rat.
But rats fear cats.
They won't get close.

Toxo changes this.
Its power is strong.
It takes away a rat's fear.
Now the rat hangs out near cats.
It likes the smell of cat urine.

You can guess what is next.
The rat gets eaten.
This is great for the toxo.
Life goes on in its new host.

9781680210316

9781680210729

9781680210484

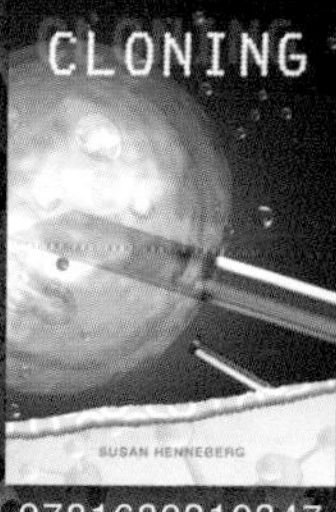

9781680210347

9781680210477

9781680210293

9781680210538

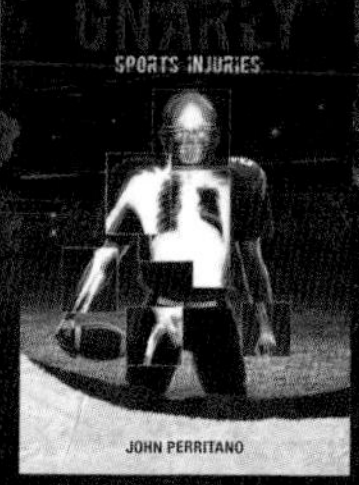

9781680210712

9781680210491

9781680210378

9781680210552

9781680210545